Selecting Mutual Funds:
How to Choose Wisely

DOUGLAS DICKEY

Copyright © 2019 Douglas Dickey
All rights reserved.
ISBN: 9781077739048

DEDICATION

For my children...Allyson, Megan, Nathan, Morgan, Emma, and Eli. May your lives become a little bit easier now that you've learned how to manage money. I never had that advantage and I pray that I've been able to give it to you. "Anything's possible if you show up"

Especially for my bride...Sara Jo. You have captured my heart and inspired me to be a better man. I've not always been able to live up to that, but I've done my best. My life would have been a sad and unproductive one without you around. You are the love of my life and that will never change. "I would rather spend one lifetime with you, than face all the ages of this world alone."

CONTENTS

1 Why Listen to Me? — 1

2 The Buffett Gamble — 5

3 The Power of Risk and Return — 10

4 Selecting Mutual Funds — 16

5 Skip the Details — 29

6 My Process for Mutual Funds — 31

7 Evaluate the Results — 40

8 401(k) vs IRA — 47

9 When to make changes — 49

10 Safety for Retirement — 53

11 Final Thoughts — 55

Why listen to me?

I am not an expert. I don't have any financial certifications. I am NOT a financial planner that will tell you where to put your money. That being said, I am educated. I have a Bachelor's degree in Information Systems and a Master's degree in Business Administration. This formal training has been an advantage as I built my career in the field of technology. But the one thing my formal education didn't teach me was how to handle money or how to invest for the future.

My parents weren't financial wizards. They made some good decisions over the course of their lives, but when I contemplated buying my first house I remember my father saying, "I'm not really the best person to give advice on that. I've lost money on every house I've ever owned." Needless to say there were not a lot of home lessons about responsible saving or spending habits. So I grew up ignorant…that is, lacking knowledge of how to move forward. I also grew up with a desire to spend beyond my means which put me about $25,000 in credit card debt in the first few years after I left college.

So why would you listen to a guy with this sort of background about finances? The reason is simple...I want to help you. Not so that you'll give me loads of thanks. Not so that you'll sing my praises to your friends. Not so that you'll send me a stipend every year for what I helped you learn. I simply want to help you. As I started down the path of learning about mutual funds there was no one to give me sage advice that didn't want something from me in return. There were insurance people who wanted to get a commission on my insurance purchases sometimes under the mask of helping me. There were financial planners who were happy to help me as long as I paid them annual fees or fees every time I wanted to invest my money. There were others who wanted to sell me expensive training programs to teach me how to invest in the market. But there was no one who gave me a simple approach to planning for the future and selecting good mutual funds that would grow over time.

In addition to wanting to help you, I wanted to help my children. I wanted to write down what I learned and give them a starting point that they will eventually expand on into the future. I wanted to leave a legacy for them that they could have money and also be generous to others in need. This "treatise", if I can call it that, includes a process for selecting mutual funds and my thoughts on when to make adjustments to a mutual fund portfolio. I'm hoping they'll find this helpful and not too dreadfully dull (as a couple of them surely will find it).

One real advantage of writing this down, and the reason you may want to peruse this short book, is that I was able to document my process for selecting mutual funds with no hidden agenda. I'm not looking to you to pay me a percentage of your assets each year to learn this information. In fact, you probably paid less for this than two cups of Starbuck's coffee. I'm not looking to hold your hand or advise you of the best way to spend your time and finances. I'm not trying to help you do estate planning. I am not trying to advise you on which specific mutual funds to select or to define "good" vs. "bad" investments. This is strictly a "How I Did It" book that's focused on providing a simple step-by-step process for picking mutual funds. When I started out, I wanted to know where I could find strong and profitable funds. This process helped me to find them.

I'm asking you to read the material and decide if you can get behind my approach. I'm asking you to spend half an hour every few months reviewing your investments and decide if you need to make a change. I don't want to replace your investment advisor. For those of us without large retirement accounts, I want to help you become less dependent (or not dependent at all) on investment advisors for choosing mutual fund investments. There's no reason why you can't do the leg work yourself and find better mutual funds than an advisor who only promotes a small group of mutual funds. The intention here is to provide information that I found enlightening and useful in building a strategy on how to invest for the future.

So if you've decided at this point that you're unwilling to move forward, the best part is that it won't hurt my feelings and you won't feel like it's a waste of your time. But if you're willing to move forward, let's get started.

The Buffett Gamble

Warren Buffett is what I call the true financial expert. Why do I think that? As of 2019, Buffett was worth about $89 billion. He knows how to manage money and he knows how to invest that money for the future. He also knows that most people don't have the time or expertise to pick individual companies to invest in. His sensitivity to that and his pragmatic approach to life make him the perfect financial coach for the everyday investor.

Listen to Buffett be interviewed and you'll hear him say the following things…

> I never know what markets are going to do. I know what markets are going to do over a long period of time. They're going to go up. But in terms of what's going to happen in a day or a week or a month, I never felt I knew it and I never felt it was important.

> Consistently buy an S&P 500 low-cost index fund. I

SELECTING MUTUAL FUNDS

think it's the thing that makes the most sense practically all of the time.

The trick is not to pick the right company. The trick is to essentially buy all the big companies through the S&P 500 and to do it consistently.

Costs really matter in investments. If returns are going to be 7% or 8% and you're paying 1% for fees, that makes an enormous difference in how much money you're going to have in retirement. *[author's note: most index funds charge around 0.3%]*

One of Buffett's most telling actions was to make a friendly wager with a group of hedge fund managers called Protégé Partners. For those who aren't familiar with "hedge" funds, a hedge fund is a partnership of investors that uses high risk methods in hopes of achieving large gains. To understand the friendly bet that Buffett made with Protégé Partners, you may need a little background.

There are mutual funds called Index Funds. An index fund tries to mimic a measurement of the market. You've probably heard about the Dow Jones Industrial index, the S&P 500 index, or the Russell 2000 index on the news or in your reading material. As an example, let's look at the S&P 500 index. The index is calculated by selecting 500 companies, adding up how much each company is worth, and then dividing it by some number which is only known by the company that started the index…Standard & Poor's. An S&P 500 index fund will only buy stock in those 500 companies.

The goal of the index fund is to match the return of the index. If the S&P 500 index goes up 2%, then the S&P 500 Index Fund should go up about 2%. Hopefully that's enough to get you started. Let's get back to the Buffett wager.

Warren Buffett bet Protégé Partners that investing in an S&P 500 Index Fund would yield a better long term result than a hedge fund since the index fund tracks the market and the fees for index funds are substantially less than a hedge fund.

How did it work? Both companies put up $320,000 into bonds that would, after 10 years, be worth $1 million. The proceeds from both companies was to go to the winner's chosen charity. The bet began at the end of 2007. In 2018, the results of the bet were widely publicized. The S&P 500 index fund had returned an average of 7.1% per year while the hedge fund had only brought an average of 2.2% per year. This average return was in spite of the massive market downturn in 2008.

<u>Why is this important?</u> It's important because it's the basis of the my investment strategy and the advice I give my kids...if the amount of money you make from your investment (minus the expenses you paid to own that investment) doesn't beat the average amount of money you could have made by investing in your preferred index, such as the S&P 500, <u>then you probably have your money invested in the wrong place.</u> There are reasons to have money in lower-returning investments, but to examine this you have to understand what finance people call the "opportunity cost of

capital."

Each investment (or "opportunity") will give you some benefit. Since you can only put your money in one spot, you will be giving up the benefits of putting your money in the other options available to you. That's the "cost". You have to compare the costs & gains between the opportunities to figure out the best place for your money. For example, if you have $1000 to invest you may choose to put it in a savings account rather than a mutual fund. Both a savings account and a mutual fund are investments that will generate money using your initial investment. When you choose to put money into a savings account, it means that you will get less money each year than if you put it in a mutual fund. That's the downside or the "cost". The upside is that some of the money put into a savings account is guaranteed by the government which makes it a far less risky investment than a mutual fund. This choice to put money into a savings account means that you knew you would make less money. It "costs" you the chance to make more money from a more lucrative investment such as a mutual fund. If you had put the money into a mutual fund, you knew that you would be taking on more risk. It "costs" you the security of the government guarantee you gave up by putting your money at a higher risk of losing it than if you had chosen the savings account.

Think of it this way...if I have to choose between a carrot or a warm, chocolate chip cookie, then I have to understand the tradeoff. The carrot is healthier but is not very satisfying on a cold day. The cost was my satisfaction, but the upside was my health. If I choose the chocolate chip cookie, then I'll feel warm and satisfied but it's empty calories that I definitely don't need. The cost was empty calories and having my blood sugars spike upwards, but the upside was that it put a smile on my face.

This comparison of which cost you'll accept (the cost of less money being generated in a savings account or the cost of potentially losing some of the money you put into a mutual fund) is a key part of deciding how to set up your retirement account. There are completely valid reasons for why you would accept either of these costs. For example, I might want to use my money in the next 6 months. In that case, I want my money in a stable, liquid account (that is, easy to get it) so that I can access it quickly without losing any of my money. If I'm not going to use the money for the next 5-10 years, then I want to put it into a mutual fund so it can grow at a higher interest rate. Mutual funds can go up and down in value depending on the day. They need long periods of time to generate the higher interest rate returns.

If you're trying to grow your account or even keep up with (or beat) inflation, your investments have to generate enough interest. That's not going to happen in savings accounts or certificates of deposit or any other very low-yielding investment.

The Power of Risk and Return

For those who have heard the terms "risk" and "reward" but don't know exactly what they mean, let me attempt to give you a simple definition for each. You need to understand these items so that you can correctly and, somewhat objectively, decide where to put your money.

Risk means the possibility that you'll lose some of your money. There could be a large risk or a small risk. Please bear in mind that no matter what a financial "expert" tells you, there's always a risk of losing your money. I'm sure there's some nervous person out there who says, "But what if I put it in my mattress or bury it in the back yard?" There's still a risk. What if the house burns down (including the mattress)? What if you forgot the exact spot where you buried your money in the back yard? What if someone knows where you stash your money and they steal it from your mattress or back yard? See...there's always a risk of losing your money.

Return means how much money you could make with a

particular investment. The return is *always* tied to the risk. The more risk you're willing to take means the greater return you could get on your money. Maybe this chart will help...

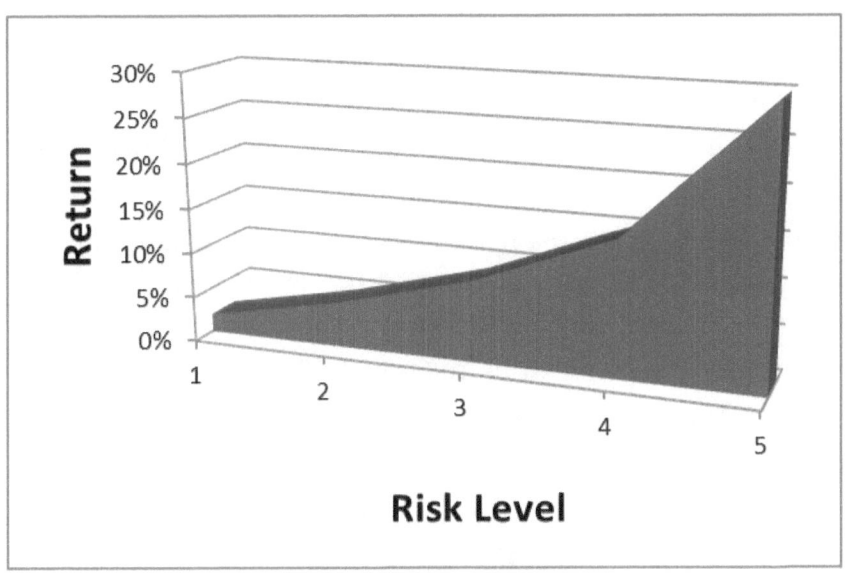

Investing in a certificate of deposit (CD) will be extremely safe and your loss is limited to the possibility that the bank goes bankrupt (extremely unlikely). However, you'll only get about half of one percent of return a year. So if you took $10,000 and bought a 12-month CD each year you'd only get $50 which you can't get to until the time limit on the CD is over without sacrificing the return you were supposed to get. On the other hand, you can invest it in stocks or stock mutual funds and get returns of 7% or more each year. The same $10,000 in stocks might yield between $700 and $2500. The best part is that you can take your return as soon as it happens. You don't have to wait.

But here's my real point about talking about Risk and

SELECTING MUTUAL FUNDS

Return. The Risk is not as risky as the media and financial planners will tell you and the Return can be less or more than you'd expect. There are many articles out there by somewhat inept financial planners (aka, sales people) that will tell you to only put your money into investments that match your "risk tolerance." In other words, if you're scared of losing any money you've worked hard to save, your risk tolerance is low…you are <u>risk-averse</u>. If you're less worried about losing money and want to see it grow more quickly, then your risk tolerance is high…you are <u>risk-tolerant</u>.

Categorizing investors this way teeters on the verge of being criminal and does a huge disservice to the investor. If the inept advisor identifies me as risk-averse, he has been taught to steer me toward lower risk investments. Because that's in my best interest? No. Because that's the wisest choice in the long run? No. Rather, it's because that's he believes I will buy. It doesn't matter if it's the right choice for me…just sell me whatever low-yielding, unimpressive investment I will buy. Just try to get that 1%-3% kickback once I buy something. Thirty years of that approach would require me to keep working late into my 70's and 80's just to make ends meet.

Every year, the company I work for has once or twice a year meetings with the investment firm that manages our 401(k) accounts. The agenda of the meeting is to let people know they can ask for advice from this group and to also discuss the importance of investing in the 401(k) using the small handful of mutual funds offered by the firm that supports the 401(k). I always attend these, in spite of my higher than average experience with mutual funds, to ensure that there's not something new I should understand to make that investment useful. I bring this up because I'm amazed at the lack of knowledge from professional people when it comes to the <u>basics</u> of investing through 401(k)s. I'm also surprised that the advice given by the financial firm matches what I just described. Keep in mind they are providing this "free" advice as part of the package they sell to your company to manage the 401(k)s.

The presenter standing in the front of the room tells everyone they have to determine their risk tolerance to decide which investments will be best for them. So if I'm risk averse, I should pick safer, lower-performing investments because I'm nervous about what's happening in the market?? How can that be a good yardstick I use to determine where the best place is to put my money? Also, the presenter tells us that if we're not going to evaluate the performance of our 401(k), we should use one of their handy-dandy "target" mutual funds. These target funds will use an algorithm based on my age to determine each year where my money should be invested and how much should go to safe investments versus riskier investments. Target mutual funds are a nice idea but they essentially tell the employee of the company that someone is going to pick their investments based on their age rather than an assessment of their personal financial situation. Again, I would say that's an extremely poor approach to helping people with their long-term investments.

Let's go back to my point about risk not being as risky as the media and financial planners tell us. The media loves to sound the alarm when the stock markets are going down. They do it often and they are very loud about it. But when the environment is more stable (which is most of the time), they don't even mention it. Why? Because the media wants to get you excited and keep you watching their TV show or reading their online postings. Fear generates a lot of buzz. But when there's nothing to scream and cry about, the media moves on to something else that will cause you to get outraged, scream, and cry.

The value of stocks and the stock market have consistently gone up over the long term. As the quote from Warren Buffet mentioned earlier in this book, we can expect the value of stocks in the market are going to go up. We also know that the stock market moves up and down every day. This means that if you need money next week, you should probably move it to a more stable or liquid investment such as your checking account so that it's available when you need it. It should not be in an investment that goes up and down every day. The key here is to find ways to reduce your risk while still having the chance to get a good return on your money.

At this point in the book, I'm going to make a confession. Hello…my name is Doug and I'm a mutual fundaholic (*Hi Doug*). That means that I'd rather put my money into a mutual fund that spreads it across 30 or more companies than I would buying stock or bonds in a single company. By spreading my money among multiple companies through a mutual fund, I get the advantage that I will have some companies that go up in value and a few others that might go down in value.

I could do my own investing in companies I like without using a mutual fund. The problem is that I have a job and family that require a great deal of my time. I don't have the time to build, and watch, a portfolio of individual companies. Instead, I pool my money with other investors into a mutual fund that pays a manager to invest the money for us. He has a staff of people researching companies and making recommendations on which stocks to buy and which stocks to sell. He has the time because this is what he does 40+ hours each week.

But if the mutual fund manager's staff are working full time on the mutual fund, we have to pay for all of that…right? You're right, we do. That's what makes stock index funds so attractive. Let's take the S&P 500 index as an example. If I set up a mutual fund to buy every company in the S&P 500 index (there are 500 companies that make up this index), then I don't need an army of people to research new stocks. I just need enough staff on hand to keep my fund balanced among the 500 companies that make up the S&P 500 index.

Selecting Mutual Funds: What to look at and how to pick them

In this section, I'll describe the different components I review when I'm selecting a mutual fund and what values I think should be there. Let me make a disclaimer at this point. The information that follows is NOT advice for the reader. It is simply a description of what I look for when making a decision about which mutual fund should hold and build my money. I should also say that when I choose a mutual fund, I consider my process 80% technical and 20% gut instinct. It's not always as clear for me as using the numbers to select a fund. Based on the numbers between two relatively equivalent mutual funds I make a judgement call that I feel is the best. Sometimes that works out and sometimes it doesn't.

When I first started getting serious about my retirement, I looked at all various types of mutual funds that included growth stock funds, balanced funds, bond funds, etc. Because returns over time seemed higher to me in the growth stock fund group, that's where I concentrated most of my attention. I continue to look at other forms of stock funds (balanced funds, value funds, etc.), but have steered clear of funds that focus on building a steady stream of income each month or each year as I usually only find ones with lower average returns over the life of the funds. That could be a mistake, but that's the approach I've chosen and it works well for me. I also have defined various approaches of how to alter my approach once I actually retire…but that's going into my next book.

MARKET CAPITALIZATION / STYLE

Market Capitalization refers to the value of the companies in a particular mutual fund. For example, a Large Capitalization (Large-Cap) mutual fund means that the companies held in this mutual fund are worth more than $10 billion each. These tend to be very large companies where growth will happen more slowly in comparison to small companies that can grow more quickly. Think of it as how quickly a car can be turned or speed up. A small car can usually turn on a dime and go from 0 to 60 in less than 10 seconds. A large 15-passenger van will not be as nimble, but will have other advantages like more features and the ability to carry more people. In an accident, the smaller car may not be as safe while the larger vehicle usually comes with less risk to the riders in the event of a fender bender.

Mid-Size Capitalization (Mid-Cap) mutual funds typically invest in companies that are worth between $2 billion and $10 billion. These companies tend to have slightly more volatility (how quickly and how often their stock price goes up and down…think riding through hills rather than driving on a relatively straight or steady incline road) than Large-Cap companies. But with the extra volatility, you can sometimes get better growth as it's easier to grow a $2 billion company than a $100 billion company.

Small Capitalization (Small-Cap) mutual funds typically invest in companies that are worth less than $2 billion. They tend to have a lot of volatility (their value goes up and down quickly like a roller coaster). But their price of their stock can go up quickly or dramatically over time. Think about the companies that were once Small-Cap and you're kicking yourself 20 years later. I remember a small company called Microsoft in the early 1980s that I thought was good, but they weren't huge. If I had invested a few hundred dollars back then, I probably could have sold those shares and retired early. Small-Cap companies don't always take off like Microsoft or Dell, but if they do the value of a mutual fund can go up quickly.

When choosing a stock mutual fund, I try to make sure I pick different varieties. I try to keep my portfolio balanced so that I've got about 40% Large-Cap, 40% Mid-Cap, and 20% Small-Cap funds. This reduces the volatility of my overall portfolio. Is it always perfectly balanced? No. But my goal is to have it close to those numbers. I also don't turn a blind eye to a mutual fund I find that has great returns over the past 20 years just because it will unbalance my portfolio. I just use these numbers as a guideline.

INCEPTION DATE

The inception date references the year the mutual fund started. I only look at mutual funds that have at least a 10-year track record. This is also one of those stats where I believe the longer the mutual fund has been around with a higher average rate of return, the better. It usually means the mutual fund manager knew what he was doing both in bull markets (when stocks go up significantly) as well as in bear markets (when stocks go down significantly).

NET EXPENSE RATIO

I see this as the "cost" of owning the mutual fund. If expenses are too high, the return has to be higher than other mutual funds to justify buying it. That's why there's been such a focus on Index Mutual Funds over the past few years. When their expenses are down around 0.3%, you will want to compare that with the expenses of a "normal" fund which typically ranges from 0.5% to 2.0%. Personally, I wouldn't mind a mutual fund that has higher fees as long as I'm rewarded with a higher return.

For example, if my S&P 500 index fund gains 8% in value, I would expect a normal fund with higher expenses to bring in 10%-14% gains. Not many can do this though some can outshine an index fund. When I find rare gems like this, I tend to put some money into them.

TRANSACTION FEE

There are mutual funds that charge a "transactional" fee. This is usually a fixed dollar amount (let's say about $75) that you pay each time you put money into a mutual fund. Again, I don't rule out mutual funds that have transaction fees, but I'm wary of them. It also means that I expect more from them than from index funds which charge lower fees and have no transaction fees.

I suspect that these fees are charged to prevent nervous investors from going in and out of the mutual fund which, in theory, makes the mutual fund more stable. This is similar to front-end loaded mutual funds that a lot of financial advisors sell. While it covers the cost of investing your money and pays the financial advisor, another stated advantage is that this practice reduces the turnover of money in the mutual fund. Keeping dollars invested means that the investments can continue to grow instead of cashing out shares of stock at a bad time to give people their money back.

OPEN TO NEW INVESTORS

This seems obvious to include in your criteria selection, but keeping it in mind will speed up the selection process. Mutual funds periodically stop accepting investments from new investors due to multiple reasons. Typically, the reason is that the fund invests in very specific types of companies that reach a certain standard. When they have a problem finding companies that match this standard, they don't want an influx of cash that will sit on the sidelines as it affects the net asset value (NAV) price of the mutual fund and it can impact the stated returns of the mutual fund. The key point here is to avoid these in your selection process so that you don't get excited by the returns of a fund only to find out that you can't invest your money there.

AVERAGE ANNUAL RETURN

I look at four annual return indicators to gain a sense of how well the fund is doing currently and also how well the fund is doing over the long term. These indicators include the 1-year, 3-year, 10-year, and Since Inception return numbers.

The 1-year and 3-year numbers tell me how well the fund has done in comparison to other mutual funds in the same time period. I give some credence to these numbers for a couple of reasons. First, because I'm closer to retirement than many others. My money doesn't have another 40 years to grow so I want to ensure the fund is doing relatively well in the short-term.

Second, I need to know if the fund is being managed well by the current management team. Managers can have a bad year but over a 3-year period how well have they done in comparison to their peers at other mutual funds. The percentage returns themselves *don't make a difference*, but it indicates the ability of the management team.

The real numbers that I focus on are the 10-year and Since Inception returns. I will note here that I marry this information with the Manager's Tenure (which we'll look at later). Having watched the market for over 30 years and seen financial crisis and recovery, these numbers can help me understand how big an impact a negative financial crisis can have. I remember a time in the 1980s when the DOW Jones Industrial Average dropped by 500 points in a day. People were absolutely freaked out. Now, no one even discusses that event.

I think one of the best indicators is the 10-year return. People can usually remember how well or how poorly the market has performed over the past 10 years. They remember recent events and also what usually caused negative or positive moves in the stock market. These can include military conflicts overseas, troubles in the housing market, new technologies, etc. They get a sense of where the economy is going even if they're not a financial expert.

Looking at the return for funds over the last 10 years also is easier to compare mutual funds against each other rather than using the Since Inception return. That's because mutual funds started at different times. Some mutual funds began 50 years ago and some 11 years ago. If you look at the "life" of the fund, a fund with 50 years' experience may show a lower return as it may have gone through multiple mutual fund managers and multiple market downturns. An 11-year-old mutual fund usually has only one manager and usually has seen only one major market downturn (or less).

MANAGER TENURE

Manager tenure indicates how long the current mutual fund manager has been managing the fund. There are two ways of looking at tenure as a measurement for a mutual fund. You can look at both the long-term and short-term returns of the fund and try to combine that with how long the manager has been in charge. If the mutual fund has high returns over the 10-year period while the short-term returns are low and the manager hasn't been running the fund for very long, then you might be tempted to say that the manager is not doing well. On the other hand, if the short-term returns are high and the long-term returns are low, you might be tempted to say that manager is an improvement over the last guy.

The problem with both of these views is that you have to take more information into account to determine if the manager is good or bad for the mutual fund. You can evaluate market trends over the last three years and attempt to determine if there were any specific or unusual circumstances that caused the market to be higher or lower than the preceding years. You'll probably need to be a financial expert to do this.

The second way to look at tenure as a measurement is to only look at mutual funds that have managers of 10 years or more. This way, the comparison between mutual funds is clearer. You'll know that the manager in charge of the fund is responsible (good or bad) for the results of the mutual fund's performance.

MINIMUM INVESTMENT

The minimum investment number tells you the bare minimum you have to invest each time you put money into the mutual fund. Most index funds and many mutual funds will allow you to put as little as $1 each time you invest in them. Others will require substantially more.

The minimum is influenced by a couple of things. The minimum can be based on the type of mutual fund. Index funds often let you invest $1 or more into the fund each time you invest. This is a great opportunity for teens or people who have low incomes to put their meager savings to work in the market. It allows for more frequent investing and taking advantage of dollar cost averaging. Dollar cost averaging is the process of investing money over time instead of larger, less frequent investing. When you do this, you usually pay an overall lower price for your total investment. Do a web search for "dollar cost averaging" if you want more information.

The minimum can also be based on discounts and opportunities your brokerage firm offers to you. I found a mutual fund through my investment group that had very good 10-year results as well as high Since Inception results. I shared this with a friend who had his IRA at another mutual fund. He asked me about the minimum investment. I told him my minimum was $100. That afternoon, he went to his brokerage firm and typed in the symbol for the mutual fund. It turns out the minimum investment for him was $25,000. That's when I realized I had been getting a benefit from my broker I didn't even realize.

I take three lessons from this situation: first, the brokerage house didn't tell me about the special investment minimum...I had to discover it on my own. Second, not all brokerage firms are created equal. If my brokerage house is offering lowered minimums for certain mutual funds, other brokerage houses are doing the same thing. If I find a fund I like and the minimum is too high, I can look at another brokerage firm to see if I can get better opportunities. Third, when my friend gave up on the idea of investing in the mutual fund I shared with him due to the large minimum, I gave him the best piece of advice I could imagine. I told him he could actually have _two_ IRA accounts...one at each firm. Seems simple enough to me.

PORTFOLIO TURNOVER

When I first learned about portfolio turnover, I wasn't very impressed or interested. I knew that funds would buy and sell shares of different companies but didn't quite understand the impact or the cost of that. As I looked into it further, it turns out to be something that can give you some interesting insights.

Let's start with the fact that portfolio turnover measures how frequently (and how much) the fund changes its assets by buying and selling those assets. In the case of stock mutual funds, it measures how much the fund bought and sold shares of stock in a particular period. This number is going to be

<u>higher for stock mutual funds that buy and sell stock more often than other stock mutual funds.</u>

Looking at this number leads me to ask two different fundamental questions about the fund. First, how good a job did the management team do picking companies that are not only growing, but are growing consistently over time? A relatively lower turnover in a growth stock mutual fund would tell me that they've picked companies that are growing at a constant and steady rate. Instead of chasing after every new company that shows growth, they are looking at the long-term growth of a company and deciding to keep it in the portfolio because it hasn't yet "maxed" out on its ability to grow substantially. That would be a good sign for me. A higher number could indicate that they aren't very good at selecting growing companies. It tells me that their process for selecting companies to invest in lacks maturity or is based on gut instinct or intuition rather than facts. If I wanted to invest on an intuitive gut feel rather than facts, *I wouldn't have hired a money manager* to manage the mutual fund.

Second, a lower turnover rate in a growth stock fund can indicate the level of discipline the manager possesses. It means that he's more careful in selecting stocks instead of moving in and out of a company to make a few quick points on a trade like day traders do. They understand the value of the company before they invest in it and have specific targets they're trying to meet. They also know when to adjust those targets and are patient to make sure they don't cash out their position too soon.

LOADED VS. NO-LOAD

Some mutual funds are considered "loaded". This means that there's a fee to either put money in or to take money out. The fee is typically a percentage of the amount you put in or take out. Front-end load mutual funds require that you pay a percentage of your investment to the mutual fund company each time you put money into the account. You've paid on the "front end" of putting your money into the account. Back-end load mutual funds require that you pay a fee when you take money out of a mutual fund.

Based on those definitions, I would never buy a back-end load mutual fund. That's like paying an extra tax on your investment. However, while I don't usually buy mutual funds with a front-end load, I don't want to disqualify a mutual fund for that. If a mutual fund can exceed the returns of other funds (minus the cost of the initial investment), then I put them on the list for consideration.

12B-1 FEES

Some mutual funds charge a fee to the mutual fund for advertising the mutual fund. These fees are called 12b-1 fees. Again, I don't disqualify a fund for having these fees, but I think carefully before I put my money with those companies. The deciding factor for me is what is the annual performance (1-year, 3-year, 10-year, and Since Inception)? If performance is higher than most, then the mutual fund becomes a real consideration.

Skip the Details

In case you wanted to skip what you perceive as my boring analysis of each of the criterion and just want the basics, here's table showing not only a summarized list of the criteria, but also what settings I use. In the next section, I'll give you a brief description of my process of selecting a mutual fund.

Criteria	Value I look for
Market Cap/Style	Small-Cap, Mid-Cap, or Large-Cap
Inception Date	Greater than 10 years
Net Expense Ratio	Less than 1%
Transaction Fee	Less than $100
Open to New Investors	Yes
Average Annual Return: 1-year	No specific criteria
Average Annual Return: 3-year	No specific criteria
Average Annual Return: 10-year	No specific criteria
Average Annual Return: Since Inception	No specific criteria
Manager Tenure	Greater than 10 years

SELECTING MUTUAL FUNDS

Criteria	Value I look for
Minimum Investment	$100
Portfolio Turnover	Less than 50%
Front Load	Find out How Much
12b-1 Fees	Less than 0.25%

My process for mutual funds

I'm a little nervous about providing this section. I'm not concerned that someone will steal my ideas or use them to make more money than I did. I'm nervous about this section because there are thousands of people who could read this and will list a couple of hundred reasons why this process is flawed. They'll point out all the flaws in the plan in an effort to push their own agendas with others. But my intent is to share with you the process I used to select investments that, over the past 10 years, has helped me to more than quadruple my initial investment amount between 2009 and 2019...part of that by adding cash from my pocket, but mostly from selecting good mutual fund investments.

First, I begin by deciding if I want a small-cap, mid-cap, or large-cap mutual fund (see definitions for these above). I decide that based on my overall portfolio. I try to have 30% of my portfolio in small-cap funds, 30% in mid-cap funds, and 40% in large-cap funds. Experts will tell you that I'm missing a key component...International Stock Funds.

When I started out my investing plan in earnest, I found two problems with keeping international stock funds in my portfolio. First, international stock markets tend to rise and fall based on what is happening in the United States' markets. When U.S. markets do well, so do the international markets. When U.S. markets do poorly, international markets seem to tank. This is not a hard and fast rule, but is frequently true. I believe this is because author Thomas Friedman was correct. The world is flat. The world economy is much more tied together than most people imagine which means all markets will tend to go up and down together.

Second, I found that even when international stock markets were doing well, my international stock mutual funds always lagged in performance compared to my US markets. I don't mean by a little bit...I mean they lagged a LOT. It was actually a detriment to keep a strictly international fund in my portfolio.

But in case you think me a snob, I have on occasion invested in mutual funds that have an international flavor. Based on performance, I have purchased Global stock mutual funds. These funds look for the best opportunities in the U.S. and internationally. They don't limit themselves to U.S. stocks only. In theory, these should be able to take advantage of opportunities across the globe where companies are performing well. But that being said, they don't make up a significant portion of my portfolio.

Now back to the point…I decide which market cap style I want to look at based on how my portfolio is balanced. If my portfolio shows too much in large-cap funds, I'll look at either mid-cap or small-cap funds to move investments into. This is not a hard and fast rule, just a guideline I use to attempt to keep my overall account balanced as mentioned above.

Sorting in a Spreadsheet

Once I've skinnied down my results to that particular market cap and put in the other settings listed above, then I pull the list into a spreadsheet so that I can sort the list in a variety of ways. This usually lowers my list from many thousand mutual funds to a few hundred. I've removed some of the columns so that you can read the example below and get a sense of what a typical search would yield. It will also give you a chance to see the process in action. Below are actual results from my brokerage firm's research tool that I have access to use. The only thing I have changed is the names of the mutual funds that came up in the list. All the other data is actual data.

SELECTING MUTUAL FUNDS

MF *	Inception	Expense	1-year	3-year	10-year	Inception	Mgr Tenure
MF 1	3/20/2000	1.66%	6.42%	24.59%	17.09%	10.51%	18.77 yrs
MF 2	12/31/1999	1.64%	3.14%	22.45%	15.36%	9.68%	19.10 yrs
MF 3	12/13/1999	2.43%	9.14%	21.60%	19.37%	-1.21%	19.15 yrs
MF 4	10/22/1990	1.13%	16.27%	20.80%	17.84%	11.85%	23.35 yrs
MF 5	8/4/2008	0.79%	13.11%	20.73%	17.53%	11.38%	11.93 yrs
MF 6	11/1/2004	0.91%	12.98%	20.59%	17.42%	10.50%	11.93 yrs
MF 7	7/1/1998	1.23%	12.67%	20.22%	16.96%	10.66%	11.93 yrs
MF 8	12/27/1996	1.05%	5.34%	20.19%	17.31%	9.32%	5.92 yrs
MF 9	4/30/2003	1.79%	-2.29%	19.83%	17.03%	12.97%	15.77 yrs
MF 10	7/8/2008	1.40%	5.42%	19.45%	18.10%	14.58%	10.57 yrs
MF 11	2/1/2006	1.24%	5.27%	19.36%	16.32%	8.48%	13.01 yrs
MF 12	7/10/2000	1.27%	4.58%	18.52%	16.58%	7.71%	17.99 yrs
MF 13	9/30/1997	1.30%	-0.92%	17.03%	14.93%	9.71%	21.35 yrs
MF 14	8/20/1998	1.07%	-2.20%	16.87%	16.37%	11.63%	20.46 yrs
MF 15	6/12/1987	1.31%	1.69%	16.66%	15.97%	11.33%	15.54 yrs
MF 16	12/30/1994	1.29%	2.27%	15.77%	15.52%	12.77%	24.10 yrs
MF 17	12/1/1993	1.13%	3.05%	15.57%	16.70%	7.97%	10.20 yrs
MF 18	11/27/2000	1.37%	1.72%	15.21%	13.02%	5.30%	18.19 yrs
MF 19	6/30/2008	1.35%	1.24%	15.15%	13.72%	7.80%	10.59 yrs
MF 20	12/29/2000	0.84%	2.05%	15.04%	16.29%	7.31%	18.10 yrs

* MF means Mutual Fund

Figure 1

In Figure 2, I start by sorting data by the 1-year performance number with the highest numbers on top and lowest numbers on the bottom. Once that's done, I begin to use the power of the spreadsheet to give me visual indicators of the certain measurements. There's a feature my spreadsheet program has called Conditional Formatting. It will "color" cells that meet a certain criteria. As I look at the 1-year returns, I look at the middle of the list (or the median) to determine the values of the top half of the list. I've done that with the list above and it looks like this...

MF	Inception	Expense	1-year	3-year	10-yr	Inception	Mgr Tenure
MF 5	8/4/2008	0.79%	13.11%	20.73%	17.53%	11.38%	11.93 yrs
MF 6	11/1/2004	0.91%	12.98%	20.59%	17.42%	10.50%	11.93 yrs
MF 7	7/1/1998	1.23%	12.67%	20.22%	16.96%	10.66%	11.93 yrs
MF 3	12/13/1999	2.43%	9.14%	21.60%	19.37%	-1.21%	19.15 yrs
MF 1	3/20/2000	1.66%	6.42%	24.59%	17.09%	10.51%	18.77 yrs
MF 10	7/8/2008	1.40%	5.42%	19.45%	18.10%	14.58%	10.57 yrs
MF 8	12/27/1996	1.05%	5.34%	20.19%	17.31%	9.32%	5.92 yrs
MF 11	2/1/2006	1.24%	5.27%	19.36%	16.32%	8.48%	13.01 yrs
MF 12	7/10/2000	1.27%	4.58%	18.52%	16.58%	7.71%	17.99 yrs
MF 2	12/31/1999	1.64%	3.14%	22.45%	15.36%	9.68%	19.10 yrs
MF 17	12/1/1993	1.13%	3.05%	15.57%	16.70%	7.97%	10.20 yrs
MF 16	12/30/1994	1.29%	2.27%	15.77%	15.52%	12.77%	24.10 yrs
MF 20	12/29/2000	0.84%	2.05%	15.04%	16.29%	7.31%	18.10 yrs
MF 18	11/27/2000	1.37%	1.72%	15.21%	13.02%	5.30%	18.19 yrs
MF 15	6/12/1987	1.31%	1.69%	16.66%	15.97%	11.33%	15.54 yrs
MF 19	6/30/2008	1.35%	1.24%	15.15%	13.72%	7.80%	10.59 yrs
MF 13	9/30/1997	1.30%	-0.92%	17.03%	14.93%	9.71%	21.35 yrs
MF 14	8/20/1998	1.07%	-2.20%	16.87%	16.37%	11.63%	20.46 yrs
MF 9	4/30/2003	1.79%	-2.29%	19.83%	17.03%	12.97%	15.77 yrs
MF 4	10/22/1990	1.13%	-16.27%	20.80%	17.84%	11.85%	23.35 yrs

Figure 2

SELECTING MUTUAL FUNDS

I notice from Figure 2 that the median number is 4.58%. Then I use conditional formatting to highlight in green all 1-year results that are greater than or equal to 4.58%. Figure 3 shows that...

MF	Inception	Expense	1-year
MF 5	8/4/2008	0.79%	13.11%
MF 6	11/1/2004	0.91%	12.98%
MF 7	7/1/1998	1.23%	12.67%
MF 3	12/13/1999	2.43%	9.14%
MF 1	3/20/2000	1.66%	6.42%
MF 10	7/8/2008	1.40%	5.42%
MF 8	12/27/1996	1.05%	5.34%
MF 11	2/1/2006	1.24%	5.27%
MF 12	7/10/2000	1.27%	4.58%
MF 2	12/31/1999	1.64%	3.14%
MF 17	12/1/1993	1.13%	3.05%
MF 16	12/30/1994	1.29%	2.27%
MF 20	12/29/2000	0.84%	2.05%
MF 18	11/27/2000	1.37%	1.72%
MF 15	6/12/1987	1.31%	1.69%
MF 19	6/30/2008	1.35%	1.24%
MF 13	9/30/1997	1.30%	-0.92%
MF 14	8/20/1998	1.07%	-2.20%
MF 9	4/30/2003	1.79%	-2.29%
MF 4	10/22/1990	1.13%	-16.27%

Figure 3

The next step is to then sort the list by 3-year results and follow the same process of finding and highlighting the larger returns as I did with the 1-year results. Figure 4 shows the results of that effort.

MF	Inception	Expense	1-year	3-year
MF 1	3/20/2000	1.66%	6.42%	24.59%
MF 2	12/31/1999	1.64%	3.14%	22.45%
MF 3	12/13/1999	2.43%	9.14%	21.60%
MF 4	10/22/1990	1.13%	-16.27%	20.80%
MF 5	8/4/2008	0.79%	13.11%	20.73%
MF 6	11/1/2004	0.91%	12.98%	20.59%
MF 7	7/1/1998	1.23%	12.67%	20.22%
MF 8	12/27/1996	1.05%	5.34%	20.19%
MF 9	4/30/2003	1.79%	-2.29%	19.83%
MF 10	7/8/2008	1.40%	5.42%	19.45%
MF 11	2/1/2006	1.24%	5.27%	19.36%
MF 12	7/10/2000	1.27%	4.58%	18.52%
MF 13	9/30/1997	1.30%	-0.92%	17.03%
MF 14	8/20/1998	1.07%	-2.20%	16.87%
MF 15	6/12/1987	1.31%	1.69%	16.66%
MF 16	12/30/1994	1.29%	2.27%	15.77%
MF 17	12/1/1993	1.13%	3.05%	15.57%
MF 18	11/27/2000	1.37%	1.72%	15.21%
MF 19	6/30/2008	1.35%	1.24%	15.15%
MF 20	12/29/2000	0.84%	2.05%	15.04%

Figure 4

SELECTING MUTUAL FUNDS

And we do the same with 10-year returns...

MF	Inception	Expense	Transaction	1-year	3-year	10-year
MF 3	12/13/1999	2.43%	No	9.14%	21.60%	19.37%
MF 10	7/8/2008	1.40%	No	5.42%	19.45%	18.10%
MF 4	10/22/1990	1.13%	No	-16.27%	20.80%	17.84%
MF 5	8/4/2008	0.79%	Yes	13.11%	20.73%	17.53%
MF 6	11/1/2004	0.91%	Yes	12.98%	20.59%	17.42%
MF 8	12/27/1996	1.05%	No	5.34%	20.19%	17.31%
MF 1	3/20/2000	1.66%	No	6.42%	24.59%	17.09%
MF 9	4/30/2003	1.79%	No	-2.29%	19.83%	17.03%
MF 7	7/1/1998	1.23%	No	12.67%	20.22%	16.96%
MF 17	12/1/1993	1.13%	No	3.05%	15.57%	16.70%
MF 12	7/10/2000	1.27%	No	4.58%	18.52%	16.58%
MF 14	8/20/1998	1.07%	No	-2.20%	16.87%	16.37%
MF 11	2/1/2006	1.24%	No	5.27%	19.36%	16.32%
MF 20	12/29/2000	0.84%	Yes	2.05%	15.04%	16.29%
MF 15	6/12/1987	1.31%	No	1.69%	16.66%	15.97%
MF 16	12/30/1994	1.29%	No	2.27%	15.77%	15.52%
MF 2	12/31/1999	1.64%	No	3.14%	22.45%	15.36%
MF 13	9/30/1997	1.30%	No	-0.92%	17.03%	14.93%
MF 19	6/30/2008	1.35%	No	1.24%	15.15%	13.72%
MF 18	11/27/2000	1.37%	No	1.72%	15.21%	13.02%

Figure 5

And the same with Since Inception returns as in Figure 6...

MF	Inception	Expense	1-year	3-year	10-year	Inception
MF 10	7/8/2008	1.40%	5.42%	19.45%	18.10%	14.58%
MF 9	4/30/2003	1.79%	-2.29%	19.83%	17.03%	12.97%
MF 16	12/30/1994	1.29%	2.27%	15.77%	15.52%	12.77%
MF 4	10/22/1990	1.13%	-16.27%	20.80%	17.84%	11.85%
MF 14	8/20/1998	1.07%	-2.20%	16.87%	16.37%	11.63%
MF 5	8/4/2008	0.79%	13.11%	20.73%	17.53%	11.38%
MF 15	6/12/1987	1.31%	1.69%	16.66%	15.97%	11.33%
MF 7	7/1/1998	1.23%	12.67%	20.22%	16.96%	10.66%
MF 1	3/20/2000	1.66%	6.42%	24.59%	17.09%	10.51%
MF 6	11/1/2004	0.91%	12.98%	20.59%	17.42%	10.50%
MF 13	9/30/1997	1.30%	-0.92%	17.03%	14.93%	9.71%
MF 2	12/31/1999	1.64%	3.14%	22.45%	15.36%	9.68%
MF 8	12/27/1996	1.05%	5.34%	20.19%	17.31%	9.32%
MF 11	2/1/2006	1.24%	5.27%	19.36%	16.32%	8.48%
MF 17	12/1/1993	1.13%	3.05%	15.57%	16.70%	7.97%
MF 19	6/30/2008	1.35%	1.24%	15.15%	13.72%	7.80%
MF 12	7/10/2000	1.27%	4.58%	18.52%	16.58%	7.71%
MF 20	12/29/2000	0.84%	2.05%	15.04%	16.29%	7.31%
MF 18	11/27/2000	1.37%	1.72%	15.21%	13.02%	5.30%
MF 3	12/13/1999	2.43%	9.14%	21.60%	19.37%	-1.21%

Figure 6

Evaluate the results

Now I'm ready to review the information and decide where to invest my money. Figure 7 shows the final state of the table with the highlights. I've put boxes around mutual funds that have been in the top 50% of their returns in each period of time. These are the mutual funds I'm going to examine most closely.

MF	Inception	Expense	1-year	3-year	10-year	Inception
MF 10	7/8/2008	1.40%	5.42%	19.45%	18.10%	14.58%
MF 9	4/30/2003	1.79%	-2.29%	19.83%	17.03%	12.97%
MF 16	12/30/1994	1.29%	2.27%	15.77%	15.52%	12.77%
MF 4	10/22/1990	1.13%	-16.27%	20.80%	17.84%	11.85%
MF 14	8/20/1998	1.07%	-2.20%	16.87%	16.37%	11.63%
MF 5	8/4/2008	0.79%	13.11%	20.73%	17.53%	11.38%
MF 15	6/12/1987	1.31%	1.69%	16.66%	15.97%	11.33%
MF 7	7/1/1998	1.23%	12.67%	20.22%	16.96%	10.66%
MF 1	3/20/2000	1.66%	6.42%	24.59%	17.09%	10.51%
MF 6	11/1/2004	0.91%	12.98%	20.59%	17.42%	10.50%
MF 13	9/30/1997	1.30%	-0.92%	17.03%	14.93%	9.71%
MF 2	12/31/1999	1.64%	3.14%	22.45%	15.36%	9.68%
MF 8	12/27/1996	1.05%	5.34%	20.19%	17.31%	9.32%
MF 11	2/1/2006	1.24%	5.27%	19.36%	16.32%	8.48%
MF 17	12/1/1993	1.13%	3.05%	15.57%	16.70%	7.97%
MF 19	6/30/2008	1.35%	1.24%	15.15%	13.72%	7.80%
MF 12	7/10/2000	1.27%	4.58%	18.52%	16.58%	7.71%
MF 20	12/29/2000	0.84%	2.05%	15.04%	16.29%	7.31%
MF 18	11/27/2000	1.37%	1.72%	15.21%	13.02%	5.30%
MF 3	12/13/1999	2.43%	9.14%	21.60%	19.37%	-1.21%

Figure 7

You'll notice in Figure 8 some companies that have done very well over the past 10 years, but over the life of the fund (since inception) they haven't done well at all. Mutual Fund 8 and Mutual Fund 3 have good 10-year numbers, but poor "since inception" numbers in comparison to the other funds.

SELECTING MUTUAL FUNDS

MF	Inception	Expense	10-year	Inception	Mgr Tenure	Turnover	Load	12b-1
MF 8	12/27/1996	1.05%	17.31%	9.32%	5.92 yrs	43.00%	5.25%	0.25%
MF 3	12/13/1999	2.43%	19.37%	-1.21%	19.15 yrs	46.00%	0.00%	0.25%

Figure 8

In the case of Mutual Fund 8, the manager has only been in charge of the fund for the past 6 years. His short-term record is good, but he isn't responsible for either the 10-year number or the "since inception" number. In the case of Mutual Fund 3, the manager is the original manager of the fund. It appears that he made poor decisions in the early days of the fund but looks to have been turning things around over the past 10 years.

I'm using this as an example to let you know why I might pass on Mutual Fund 3. Look at the comparison of Mutual Fund 3 with Mutual Fund 1 in Figure 9. You'll notice a couple of things they have in common. First, they have both been around about the same amount of time. Second, their managers have pretty much been the only managers of the fund. But also notice the differences…a) the expense ratio on Mutual Fund one is substantially less than the expenses for Mutual Fund 3 and b) Mutual Fund 1 doesn't charge a marketing fee while Mutual Fund 3 does.

MF	Inception	Expense	10-year	Inception	Mgr Tenure	Turnover	Load	12b-1
MF 1	3/20/2000	1.66%	17.09%	10.51%	18.77 yrs	9.00%	0.00%	0.00%
MF 3	12/13/1999	2.43%	19.37%	-1.21%	19.15 yrs	46.00%	0.00%	0.25%

Figure 9

My conclusion after reviewing these two companies is that Mutual Fund 1 has given a better return over almost 20 years and charged me a full percent less than Mutual Fund 3.

That's how I weed out potential funds. But what do I do to compare the really good funds? I begin by pulling out only funds that are "green" for all four performance indicators. Let's look at the good ones in this list on Figure 10...

MF	Inception	Expense	1-year	3-year	10-year	Inception	Load	12b-1
MF 10	7/8/2008	1.40%	5.42%	19.45%	18.10%	14.58%	0.00%	0.20%
MF 5	8/4/2008	0.79%	13.11%	20.73%	17.53%	11.38%	0.00%	0.00%
MF 7	7/1/1998	1.23%	12.67%	20.22%	16.96%	10.66%	5.75%	0.25%
MF 1	3/20/2000	1.66%	6.42%	24.59%	17.09%	10.51%	0.00%	0.00%
MF 6	11/1/2004	0.91%	12.98%	20.59%	17.42%	10.50%	0.00%	0.00%

Figure 10

I would add up the expenses listed for each fund as in Figure 11.

MF	Inception	Expense	1-year	3-year	10-year	Inception	Load	12b-1	Expenses
MF 10	7/8/2008	1.40%	5.42%	19.45%	18.10%	14.58%	0.00%	0.20%	1.60%
MF 5	8/4/2008	0.79%	13.11%	20.73%	17.53%	11.38%	0.00%	0.00%	0.79%
MF 7	7/1/1998	1.23%	12.67%	20.22%	16.96%	10.66%	5.75%	0.25%	1.48%
MF 1	3/20/2000	1.66%	6.42%	24.59%	17.09%	10.51%	0.00%	0.00%	1.66%
MF 6	11/1/2004	0.91%	12.98%	20.59%	17.42%	10.50%	0.00%	0.00%	0.91%

Figure 11

Look at Figure 12 for a moment...

MF	Inception	Expense	3-year	10-year	12b-1	Expenses
MF 10	7/8/2008	1.40%	19.45%	18.10%	0.20%	1.60%
MF 5	8/4/2008	0.79%	20.73%	17.53%	0.00%	0.79%
MF 7	7/1/1998	1.23%	20.22%	16.96%	0.25%	1.48%
MF 1	3/20/2000	1.66%	24.59%	17.09%	0.00%	1.66%
MF 6	11/1/2004	0.91%	20.59%	17.42%	0.00%	0.91%

Figure 12

My first concern is expenses in comparison to how much the fund returns to me. Mutual Fund 1 and Mutual Fund 7 are more expensive than most the other funds and yet have roughly the same 10-year return. It's hard to justify the higher expenses when I could have paid lower expenses for a mutual fund that did just as well or better.

You'll notice that I pulled out the Since Inception return from the table. At this point in my analysis, I'm not as concerned about how much the fund has made since the fund was started. I'm more concerned with recent history on how the fund has performed. I won't use the Since Inception return number from this point forward. Now our table looks like this in Figure 13…

MF	Inception	Expense	3-year	10-year	12b-1	Expenses
MF 10	7/8/2008	1.40%	19.45%	18.10%	0.20%	1.60%
MF 5	8/4/2008	0.79%	20.73%	17.53%	0.00%	0.79%
MF 6	11/1/2004	0.91%	20.59%	17.42%	0.00%	0.91%

Figure 13

Now that I'm down to three mutual funds, the comparison gets easier. Mutual Fund 10 has really high expenses but is lowest among the 3-year return and only about half a percent higher in the 10-year return. It doesn't make sense to pay more money for a fund that can't significantly out-perform its peers. Strike Mutual Fund 10 from the list.

MF	Inception	Expense	3-year	10-year	12b-1	Expenses
MF 5	8/4/2008	0.79%	20.73%	17.53%	0.00%	0.79%
MF 6	11/1/2004	0.91%	20.59%	17.42%	0.00%	0.91%

Figure 14

That leaves us with two mutual funds to review. Mutual Fund 5 and Mutual Fund 6 both have almost identical statistics in terms of return, but Mutual Fund 6 has higher fees. Again, why pay higher fees for a mutual fund that does the same as a mutual fund with lower fees? So that's it! Mutual Fund 5 is our choice…or is it?

There's one more comparison to make. Remember we talked about index funds earlier and using those as a benchmark for picking mutual funds. The final step in my process is to compare the 3-yr and 10-yr returns with those of an index fund that I own.

MF	Inception	Expense	3-year	10-year	12b-1	Expenses
MF 5	8/4/2008	0.79%	20.73%	17.53%	0.00%	0.79%
S&P 500 Index Fund	5/1/1997	0.02%	9.19%	13.02%	0.00%	0.02%

Figure 15

If the index fund (which can carry an expense of as little as .25%) has the same or better returns than Mutual Fund 5, then I'm better off investing in the index fund. Once I complete that comparison, then I'm done! I invest my money in what I believe is the correct mutual fund and walk happily down the road.

There is one final caveat to this method that bears mentioning. Past performance is NOT a guarantee of future success. In other words, just because Mutual Fund 5 did a great job over the past 10 years does not mean that it will do well this year or next year or the year after that. That's the gamble you take with the stock market. But even then, the market has continued to grow over the past 100 years. It's a solid tool for building a retirement for yourself.

401(k) vs. IRA

This will be a short section. Should you invest all your retirement into a 401(k) or IRA? The answer is a little bit of both where possible. Let's look at the following steps to take in where to place your money. Follow these four steps:

1. If your company matches your 401(k) investment, then invest enough money in your Roth 401(k) to get the full company match. The company will put their portion of your retirement into a traditional 401(k). Then, move to step 2.

2. Put the full amount possible into a Roth IRA (do not use a traditional IRA). At the time of this writing for people under 50, you can put in up to $6000. People age 50 and older can put in up to $7000. The limits change periodically, so you'll want to search the web for the most current limits. Once you reach this limit, go to step 3.

3. If after steps 1 and 2 you still have money you'd like to put towards retirement, then put the remaining amount in your Roth 401(k). If your company doesn't offer a Roth 401(k), put the remaining amount into a Traditional 401(k). At the time of this writing, you can contribute up to $19,000 total into your 401(k).

SELECTING MUTUAL FUNDS

4. If you've maxed out your Roth IRA and your Roth 401(k) and you still have money to invest, open a regular account at the same company where you keep your IRA and invest the remainder there.

When to Make Changes

A friend asked me to include this section in my book. The question he posed was, "After I pick my mutual funds, how often should I re-evaluate their performance and make changes?" I find that a daunting question. When I was younger (more time left until retirement), I was able to be more patient and perhaps a bit too forgiving of bad performance by a mutual fund manager. I was pretty firm on the idea that each fund would get at least a full year to prove itself. However, now I watch each fund's performance in relation to benchmark indicators (the S&P 500 or the Russell 2000).

But let's step back for a minute and talk about the following: how to track the performance of your funds to see progress; how often you might want to check your portfolio; how to evaluate the performance of the funds; and when you should actually make changes.

Tracking Performance

Tracking a mutual fund's performance can be done a couple of different ways. The first way would be through your brokerage firm. The problem with using their reporting is that it's very limited and not suited to reviewing your performance throughout the course of the year. Reporting that is specific to my investments only shows me the performance for the previous day breaking down each mutual fund and describing in either dollars or percentages how the fund did that day. There's not really long-term reporting available. I can pull down files of all my transactions or I can review my quarterly statements, but that's about it. This lack of flexibility makes relying on your brokerage firm a bad idea in my opinion.

A second way to track your funds' performance is to use the tried and true method of putting your information into a spreadsheet program. It can be as easy as tracking the last current numbers and comparing them to what you had at the beginning of the year. If you have multiple mutual funds, most brokerage firms will let you download information about your account into a format that a spreadsheet can read so you don't have to enter all the numbers manually. If you don't know much about spreadsheets, you'll want to learn to how to use them so you can track the information and use a few formulas for calculating the return on your investments.

How Often to Check Your Portfolio

This is where it gets interesting. Let's start with a reality gut-check. Are you impulsive? Are you nervous about your money being in the market? Are you risk-averse (this is the one time it's ok to ask that question)? If the answer to one or more of these questions is yes, then I would say that you only need to check it once every 3-to-6 months. I wouldn't recommend going more than 6 months without checking in on your investments. Please keep in mind that checking the status and value of your mutual funds doesn't mean you have to "do" something. You can just check in and see if you need to evaluate further.

If you didn't answer yes to those questions, then you may be ok checking it more often…perhaps weekly or even daily. This requires more self-discipline. Some who check their accounts frequently are inclined to close out certain mutual funds after a few days of declines. You want to be careful that you don't make rash decisions based on a few days of market data. Deciding if you should do something is covered in the next subsection of this chapter. Personally, I check my account more than once a week. A friend of mine calls this my version of "fantasy football". I enjoy watching what's happening with my account. 99.9% of the time, I don't make any changes. I just like to watch it.

How to Evaluate Your Mutual Fund's Performance

This is an easy section for me to write. I look at two things when deciding to cash out a mutual fund. First, I compare the performance of the mutual fund with the benchmark I'm tracking (e.g., S&P 500). If the performance of your benchmark fund exceeds the mutual fund, it's probably time to cash it out and either put it into a benchmark index fund or find a different mutual fund. Be cautious when making this choice. Make sure you're comparing the performance of your mutual fund with the right benchmark. For example, if you're looking at a large company mutual fund, you might compare it to the S&P 500 Index. If you're looking at a small company mutual fund, you might want to compare it to the Russell 2000 index which tracks smaller companies.

Second, I compare my similar mutual funds to each other. If one fund does badly over the course of a few weeks, a month, or a quarter, but other mutual funds that are similar in where they invest money are doing well, that tells me the mutual fund manager is making mistakes that no one else is making. Here's an example: If I have a large company mutual fund that is down 1.3% for the past three months but my other large company mutual funds are up 2.1%, it's time to make a change.

I was once told that, "Mutual funds don't work like that. You're supposed to stay with them for several years." I told that person (who worked for a financial planner's office) that if the mutual fund manager doesn't do as well as everyone else in the market, I was certainly not going to allow him to invest my money. I'm responsible for where my money is invested…not the mutual fund manager who is pulling in a high 6-figure salary while I take financial losses.

Safety for Retirement

If there's risk in putting my money into the stock market, then shouldn't I put money into other investments to "protect my wealth"? I wish it were an easy answer, but it's not. However, I do have a few thoughts.

First, you need wealth to protect before you worry about this. If you've got less than $100,000, then you don't need to worry about putting money into vastly different types of investments. Unless you've got a pile of cash sitting in a checking or savings account, it's unlikely that you could safely or wisely invest in other areas like Real Estate.

Second, if all your assets (savings for retirement) are in a 401(k) or IRA, some will advise you to only choose lower-yielding investments like Bond Mutual Funds (Bond Funds) or Real Estate Investment Trusts (REITs). While there's nothing wrong with these approaches, they won't yield as much return in the long run. They may make your retirement money "stable" but it won't be growing very quickly. If you've got $2+ million, then this might be a good approach for you. For those of us who won't have over $2 million (or even $1 million) when we retire, we need a way for our money to

SELECTING MUTUAL FUNDS

continue to grow and offset inflation.

Finally, as we discussed earlier, you have to understand risk versus reward as that will drive your decisions. If you've got a small amount of money that you need to continue to grow during your retirement, you'll need to put it into a "riskier" investment like Growth Stock Mutual Funds. These may have periods of downturns, but they will always come back and they will continue to grow your money at a rate that will ultimately outpace inflation. On the other hand, if you've got a very large sum and you can live off the interest of 3% to 6% each year, then you can afford to take a less risky investment like a bond fund or a REIT as you don't need your money to grow during retirement.

Final Thoughts

Everything in life comes back to personal responsibility. As I said above, I'm responsible for my financial future...not my boss or my friends or my financial planner or the manager of the mutual funds I own. Too many people are willing to turn over their money and their future to those who have agendas rather than rolling up their sleeves and understanding what needs to be done.

You're probably thinking, "I can't become knowledgeable in everything. There's too much." I understand that sentiment. But for those who have been around the block awhile, I would say that you took time to learn about health insurance when you had to pay your doctor. You learned the basics of buying a house. You figured out how to drive a car. These are all essential things for living your life. When you let them slide, you're in for some nasty surprises.

Take the time to learn some basics. Don't try to be an expert (I'm certainly not), but make sure you understand some of the basics and some basic vocabulary. You can do it by spending a couple of hours every three to six months.

On the dedication page of this book, I included the quote, "Anything's possible if you show up." If you "show up" and gain the knowledge you need, you can dramatically change the shape of your family tree. You can learn what you need to know. You can take control of your money. Try to keep an eye on your future…it will come way too soon. Best of Luck to you!

www.ingramcontent.com/pod-product-compliance
Lightning Source LLC
Chambersburg PA
CBHW030019190526
45157CB00016B/3137